What do we mean by

Cornwall is a magical, historic place – a land
of saints. The rocky skeleton gives us a beau
uplands and the proximity of the Gulf Stream a tempered climate.

Cornwall's landscape is the result of human history as well as natural history acting on the land. With the changing seasons and surge of the sea man has built, fished, mined and farmed this ancient land. The result is a landscape of contrasts; of old industry and intensive farming, expansive moors and tangled woods. All of these contribute to the sometimes rugged and sometimes serene feelings experienced as you explore the county. The unique wildlife has adapted with time to these changes and thrives in the expected places but in plenty of unexpected ones too. No longer do we think of Wild Cornwall as the chunks of land untouched by man but of the glorious interactions between man and nature. This book is your introduction to the renaissance of Wild Cornwall.

How to use this book

This guide is designed to help you explore Cornwall's landscape in a different way. To aid your discovery of Wild Cornwall each landscape type is given a broad introduction and then selected sites are described in detail.

The idea is to enable the reader to recognise a landscape type, to understand a little about it, and know what wildlife might be just around the corner. Wherever you are you will be able to find Wild Cornwall.

The locations of these landscapes are shown on the map inside the back cover and these are colour coded by chapter to make your exploration as effortless as possible. Also included is useful information on how to get there, car parking, and the nearest toilets, pubs and shops.

We have tried to make this guide as informative, accurate and usable as possible, but please contact wildlife@edenproject.com with any comments.

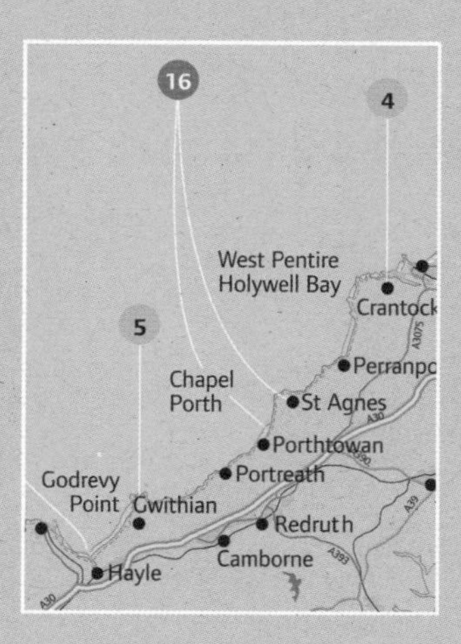

Getting around

Many of the best places to see wildlife in Cornwall are away from the main roads and difficult to reach by public transport. We understand that most of you will be in cars, but we hope that you might walk, cycle or use buses where possible.

Bus timetables can be obtained from First (01209) 719988, Truronian (01872) 273453, Western Greyhound (01637) 871871 and for general public transport enquiries contact Traveline (0870) 608 2608.

Dunes and cliffs

Cornwall is a magnificent peninsula jutting into mild seas and the beautiful coastline is never far away. From the high central peaks of Rough Tor, Carn Brea or Brown Willy the north and south coasts can be seen glinting in the distance.

The north coast is rugged and magical with secret coves hidden between giant cliffs and sprawling sandy bays. Conversely, the south coast is more sheltered with rolling wooded valleys and estuaries. Some of the most extraordinary habitats in Wild Cornwall are the extensive dune systems, magnificent cliffs and seashore.

Coastal exposure in Cornwall is permanent as wild seas, strong winds and salty air assault the coast. Man has a significant impact too. Walkers, golfers, the army, scientists and many more play a part in the shaping of these landscapes and the conservation of wildlife.

Sea holly

Dunes

Marram grass

The north coast is fringed with miles of sandy beaches, many of which are backed by sand dune systems. The dune sand contains seashells, ultimately, producing alkaline, infertile dune soils. Tough marram grass colonises the mobile dunes by the sea, which develop into a series of more stable, fixed 'grey' dunes. Here a rich variety of lime-loving plants thrive. In the past, dunes were usually used for rough grazing and their low productivity made them vulnerable to building development. However, other uses such as well managed golf courses and some military training areas can help to preserve wild areas of dune habitat.

Dunes

Dune systems are naturally mobile – tending to cover then re-expose many of man's impacts with time, such as mine workings and famously, old churches including St Gothian's chapel at Gwithian, St Piran's oratory at Perranporth and St Enodoc at Trebetherick. Dune management techniques concentrate on leaving the systems alone rather than stabilising eroded areas with marram grass, whilst keeping an eye on over-use by tourists, horse-riders and motorcyclists.

DON'T MISS...

Over a fifth of the plant species in Cornwall occur in dune systems. Keep an eye out for cowslips and pyramidal orchids in the spring, sea spurge, sea holly, and the very rare early gentian. Some plants such as the gorgeous marshmallow-coloured sea bindweed help stabilise moving dunes. Skylarks nest on dunes with the males marking their territories by hovering above it as they sing. Many species of butterflies fill the skies and feed on the flowers whilst adders may be found basking on the hot sands in summer.

Adder

Poppies and yellow corn marigolds

WHILE YOU ARE HERE...

Explore the fantastic beaches and climb the headland at West Pentire beyond Holywell Bay. The fields here are managed by the National Trust as a reserve for wildflowers of arable fields. Enjoy the great fields of nodding red poppies, cheery yellow corn marigolds and pink weasel's-snout in high summer.

GETTING THERE

Catch a First bus from Newquay to Perranporth (SW 757542), Holywell Bay (SW 767588) or Crantock (SW 790605). Perranporth is served by Truronian from Truro. By car follow signs from the A3075 and use the accessible National Trust car parks at Holywell Bay, Polly Joke and Crantock. Nearby, Perranporth has many pubs, toilets and shops.

USEFUL CONTACTS

For access to the military training area, contact the Commandant at Penhale Training camp, (01637) 832001.

Celtic cross

Penhale Towans to Crantock

This is the largest dune system in Cornwall, running over 4 miles (7km) along the coast between Perranporth and Crantock. These dunes rise like mini mountains. Some reach 60m, are among the highest in the country, and support a wonderful diversity of wildlife assisted by grazing from the resident rabbit population. Penhale Camp is a 380-hectare military training area. Access to the site is restricted: watch out for the red flags that warn of firing, but you are safe on the coast path. As well as the natural beauty there is plenty for families to do in the area with beaches, a fun park and golf courses close at hand.

What's about?

Look for the iconic Celtic cross, which stands near the site of St Piran's oratory, currently buried in the sand to preserve it. It is said St Piran was thrown from an Irish cliff in a great storm with a millstone tied to his neck. The storm abated and he floated across the sea on the millstone with the cross marking his landing point in Cornwall. St Piran is the patron saint of tin miners and is believed to have founded the tin industry from the confines of his cave. Subsequently, this dune area was widely mined for the mineral riches underfoot including copper, iron and lead. Very little remains visible, having being buried by sand, but dense gorse patches mark the locations of some old mine sites. The vegetation is mainly marram and fescue grasses, and the area is home to the largest colony of silver-studded blue butterflies in the county.

Gwithian sand dunes

Gwithian Towans

Gwithian Towans (*towan* means *dune* in Cornish) is the second largest dune system in Cornwall and has a dynamic history. The ancient community of Conerton was centred on the chapel of St Gothian until the shifting sands finally engulfed it. Rediscovered in 1827, St Gothian's Chapel – one of the oldest parish churches in Britain – has been buried at least three times under the shifting sands. The ruins of the National Explosives Company are visible here. Established in 1888, the last explosive made here was for use during World War 1. There is still evidence of a network of single-line rails leading from the dynamite factory to individual sand 'bunkers' where the explosives were kept.

What's about?
All that remains of the once thriving National Explosives Company on the towans is a fascinating mosaic of tramways and bunkers, now surrounded by a wealth of plants, insects and birds. The shocking blue viper's bugloss or the poisonous yellow-horned poppy bring colour to local dune systems. Pyramidal orchids flowering in early summer have distinctive purple flowers arranged in a dense pyramid. This orchid needs a calcareous substrate and so is only found on dunes and coastal blown sand in Cornwall.

Wingless, female glow-worms signal to the flying males in the summer. Glow-worms are in fact a beetle and the 'glow' is caused by a chemical reaction. Watch out for common lizards basking in the grass and sand martins darting in and out of their sand-cliff nest holes in summer.

WHILE YOU ARE HERE...

Head north to encounter spectacular coastal scenery along the coast path and visit the Cornwall Wildlife Trust Nature Reserve at Upton Towans, which is only a short walk south from the Gwithian Towans car park.

GETTING THERE

Take the B3301 coast road north of Hayle. Take a left turn after 2 miles and follow signs for the car park (SW 578407) or take the South West Coast Path from Hayle (ample parking), Godrevy (National Trust parking) or North Cliffs.

USEFUL CONTACTS

Upton Towans Reserve
c/o Cornwall Wildlife Trust,
(01872) 273939.

Pyramidal orchid

Common dolphin

Cliffs

Cornwall's cliffs are very important for their bird and plant communities and of great interest geologically. Cliff vegetation is fully exposed to wet, salty blasts from the sea and crops do not grow well. Instead, farmers used the land as rough grazing and this influenced the plant communities of the coast paths, resulting in wildflower-rich swards. In the last 50 years stock management changes and less hardy livestock resulted in poorer wildlife communities. Leaving the habitat untouched reduced the diversity of wildlife: without grazing by hardy livestock, botanical thugs such as gorse, willow and longer grasses can take over the rich, mixed, short grassland. These changes were responsible for the temporary loss of the large blue butterfly and the chough in the county. Happily, both these species have recently returned to some of their former haunts.

WHILE YOU ARE HERE...

Visit the beach and dunes of Daymer Bay, where the very rare marsh helleborine flowers from June to September, and the church of St Enodoc, burial place of the Poet Laureate, Sir John Betjeman.

GETTING THERE

Park at either of the National Trust car parks of Pentire Farm (SW 937802) or the Lead Mines (SW 941800), or walk from Polzeath beach (SW 936788). Polzeath is served by a bus service from Wadebridge and has easily accessed toilets, pubs and shops.

USEFUL CONTACTS

Seasonal North Cornwall District Council Marine Wildlife Warden, (01208) 863181.

Large blue

The Rumps and Pentire

The coastal drama of Cornwall is perhaps best at Pentire Point and the Rumps, near Polzeath. The towering cliffs descend to the deep blue of the Atlantic Ocean below; while on the cliff tops coastal plants and animals thrive. As well as stunning wildlife this site is important archaeologically, highlighting centuries of human use. On the neck of the headland unmistakable humps and hollows mark the site of an Iron Age fort. The area has been owned by the National Trust since 1936 ensuring little development has taken place and the area remains rich in wildlife and archaeological heritage. Grazing is an important aspect of the ecology of cliff-top grasslands and here animals can pass through holes in the stone hedges to graze the glorious cliff tops and headlands.

What's about?

The pinks of thrift and sea campion, spring squill, kidney vetch and the mellow aroma of wild thyme adorn the grassland. Bright perfumed bluebells grow in sheltered valleys on the east side of the Rumps in spring. Usually found in woods, the high humidity and lack of competition here allows them to flourish on the cliffs. New additions are the presence of grazing ponies and fences.

Through the work of an innovative project, many of the landowners from here to Bude are united in a scheme to improve the wildlife value of the coastal strip. An initial success of this improved management is the large blue butterfly, which is returning in small numbers to well managed areas of the coast.

Predannack Cliff, The Lizard

The Lizard possesses some of the most remarkable geology in the world. The area was at the centre of a collision between two super-continents, resulting in a unique assemblage of rocks, some of which are rarely found on the earth's surface. One example of this is serpentine, which is typically found only in the earth's mantle. This patchwork is complemented by gabbro, pillow lavas and schists. As these varied rocks are weathered different soils are produced and many diverse plant communities can be supported.

The areas in and around Predannack are owned by the National Trust and English Nature, which ensures effective conservation of the natural history. When farmers removed their livestock from these cliffs they became smothered by grass and gorse. This choked the smaller, less vigorous plants, reduced biodiversity and active conservation measures were required. In 1982, the National Trust introduced 20 bullocks to graze on the cliff. The next year the first green-winged orchid seen for decades flowered and annually hundreds of these glorious flowers cover the sward in spring. Shetland ponies and Soay sheep patrol the land controlling grass and gorse growth, allowing some of the rarer plants of The Lizard, including land quillwort and wild chives to flourish once more.

Highland cattle

What's about?

In spring the most widespread flowers on The Lizard will be thrift, sea campion and spring squill giving a mosaic of colours. Other rare flowers include the wonderfully named hairy greenweed, the parasitic thyme broomrape and fringed rupturewort. In summer chamomile covers Predannack Head, releasing a heady scent into the air. Gannets, manx shearwaters and ravens can often be seen and rock pipits breed on the cliffs. This patch of coastline is also one of the locations where the pride of Cornwall's bird community, the chough, can be found.

Kynance cove

Thyme broomrape

WHILE YOU ARE HERE...

Explore the wonderful heathland that covers much of the peninsula in purple and gold glory.

GETTING THERE

Catch a bus from Helston to Kynance Cove (June to Oct) and walk 2 miles north along the coast path.

Alternatively, park at Predannack Wollas (SW 668160) in a National Trust car park or walk from Mullion village, where you may find restaurants and pubs, along Predannack Downs, which offers easy walking to Predannack Cliff.

USEFUL CONTACTS

National Trust Lizard Countryside Office, (01326) 561407
English Nature National Nature Reserve Office, (01326) 240808.

Chough

Return of the chough

After being absent from the cliffs of Cornwall for so long the chough has finally come home. In 2001 three birds made the short trip from France and set up home on the Lizard. The following year a pair bred and so this Cornish favourite returned. The youngsters were watched round the clock by volunteers and very soon a new generation took to the skies. The first few years will be a struggle for such a small population of birds but there is confidence that the population will increase and with effective habitat management and monitoring the emblem of Cornwall will be a common sight once more.

Seals

Amazing facts

Jellyfish are often abundant around the coast in the summer months. Marine turtles, such as leatherbacks, may be seen feeding on them.

Auks, including the occasional puffin, can be seen around the cliffs near Boscastle between May and July.

Glow-worms will light your way along dune paths on warm summer evenings.

Choughs are nesting on cliffs on the Lizard for the first time in 50 years.

Puffin

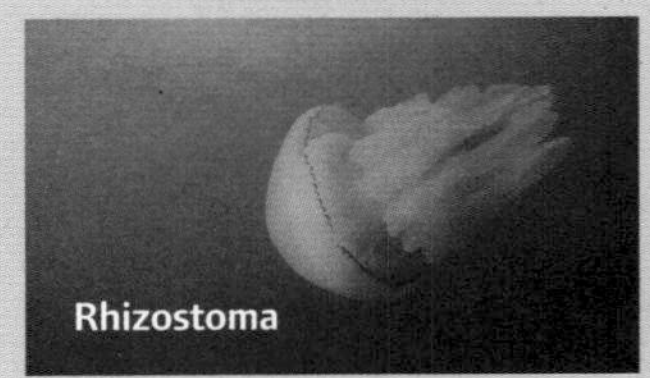

Rhizostoma

Powerful waves shape the coastline over decades

SEASONAL INTEREST

Jan	Feb	March	April	May	June	July	Aug	Sept	Oct	Nov	Dec
				Basking sharks							
				Choughs nesting							
						Heathland in flower					
				Puffins, Guillemots and Razorbills							
			Thrift								
					Orchids						

Where rivers meet the sea

Most of Cornwall's estuaries are technically rias, flooded river valleys, formed when the sea level rose after the last ice age. Those found in Cornwall are some of the cleanest and best examples of this rich habitat in the country and are incredibly important places for wildlife.

Kingfisher

Velvet swimming crab

DON'T MISS...

Listen for the curlews, and look for egrets, herons and kingfishers. Tracks or holes on the surface of the mud and sand are signs of what lives below; worms, shellfish and sea potatoes. These invertebrates form the main food source for many nationally and internationally important populations of birds and commercially important fish, such as bass, which use estuaries as nursery grounds. Otters use estuaries as feeding grounds and you may see their holts or resting places, or even see one of these elusive creatures for yourself. Estuarine shellfish are farmed and harvested for human consumption and have been for centuries. Eelgrass beds are rare nationally but grow in many Cornish estuaries and form an important habitat for estuarine wildlife.

Cornish estuaries have provided a hub for commercial and recreational activities for centuries. Hayle Estuary on the north coast, within spectacular surroundings, has been a historical focus for settlement and maritime trade and is the most south-westerly estuary in the UK. As far back as the Bronze Age the river area was used by Irish and Breton ships trading tin. As tin was used for the making of bronze tools and weapons, the activity went on into the Iron Age.

Since the mid-18th century it developed into one of Cornwall's main industrial ports, serving surrounding mines and becoming home to the Cornish Copper Company and two of Cornwall's three largest iron foundries.

The Tamar Estuary is an extensive wetland of significant wildlife conservation importance, 1,441 hectares of its area is designated as a Site of Special Scientific Interest (SSSI), and one of the biggest natural harbours in the world. Important habitats include saltmarsh surrounded by tidal mudflats and rocky shores. These areas provide a valuable haven for wintering wildfowl and waders including avocet, black-tailed godwit, curlew, dunlin, redshank and whimbrel.

Tamar Estuary

Kelp bed

Helford Estuary

The Helford Estuary is renowned for having a rich diversity of habitats and species, from the rocky shores of Rosemullion Head, to the sheltered, wooded valleys of Polwheveral and Frenchman's creeks. It was designated a Voluntary Marine Conservation Area (VMCA) to encourage local people to help protect this beautiful estuary and its wildlife treasures. The Helford is an important bass nursery area as well as being an oyster farming region, signifying the commercial importance of estuaries and their sustainable management.

The Helford has a healthy eelgrass population, which in turn provides a home for young fish, cuttlefish and even seahorses.

What's about?

On a crisp, misty spring day walk from Helford village around Frenchman's creek, made famous in Daphne du Maurier's novel of the same name, and watch herons, egrets and shelduck feed on the edge of the aromatic, squelching, chocolate brown mudflats. From May to October bass are in the estuary and in the autumn witness the raucous arrival of divers, grebes, gulls and waders that over-winter on the productive feeding grounds.

Explore the rockpools of Prisk Cove at Rosemullion, each one like a natural aquarium, filled with glorious seaweeds and animals.

WHILE YOU ARE HERE...

Visit the nearby Fal estuary system that has many wonderful creeks to explore. Most of the Fal is an important bass nursery area, oyster fishery and vitally important for its maerl beds. Maerl is a species of calcified red seaweed that can form deep deposits overlain with a thin layer of living pink maerl. This habitat suffers because of dredging and unsustainable harvesting for use as a soil conditioner, animal food additive and use in the pharmaceutical industry. Conservationists are campaigning to stop this dredging.

GETTING THERE

Catch a bus from Helston or Falmouth to Helford village. From Helston take the B3293 to St. Keverne. Turn left after 5 miles and follow the signs for Helford. The carpark is on the right before the village (SW 759262), which has accessible public toilets and pubs.

USEFUL CONTACTS

Helford VMCA, c/o Cornwall Wildlife Trust, (01872) 273939.

Lobster

WHILE YOU ARE HERE...

Visit the National Lobster Hatchery in Padstow, explore the cliffs and beaches nearby and catch the ferry to Rock to experience panoramic views of this expansive estuary.

GETTING THERE

Catch the bus from Bodmin Parkway train station to Wadebridge or Padstow. Accessible car parking is found in Wadebridge (SW 988726) and Padstow (SW 915754). Follow the brown tourist signs to the trail to begin your exploration. There are many easily found and accessed pubs and public toilets in the harbour of Padstow and Wadebridge town centre.

USEFUL CONTACTS

Camel Trail Contact Helpline, (01872) 327310
SUSTRANS – The National Cycle Network, (0117) 929 0888 or info@sustrans.org.uk.

Little egret

Camel Estuary

The River Camel begins life as a small brook high on Bodmin Moor. After passing through Wadebridge the Camel opens out into a glorious estuary with huge exposed mudflats, reed beds, creeks and pools. The estuary fills the great expanse between Padstow and Rock on the rugged north coast of Cornwall and is used today for water sports, fishing and mussel farming.

The entire estuary is accessible by the Camel Trail. This public bike and footpath follows the route of the old Atlantic Coast Express and allows for stunning views of the estuary and wildlife. Monuments to the past enrich the journey such as the spectacular iron bridge near Padstow and numerous cuttings, platforms and sidings. Old slate quarries 360 feet deep mark the half-way point between Wadebridge and Padstow and highlight the mineral heritage of Cornwall. Now filled with water and wildlife they are rumoured to contain the hulking wrecks of World War II tanks.

What's about?

As the gravel trail crunches underfoot keep your senses alert for the local wildlife, including otters, dragonflies and many bird species. Listen for the flocks of wading birds, such as curlew, and spy elegant little egrets, delicately searching for food in the shallows. In the creeks large shoals of mullet can be found, every fish glinting in the shallow sunlit waters. Flounder are well camouflaged against the sand or mud bottom where they feed on worms and other invertebrates.

Further upstream in the shady wooded areas look for kingfishers, dippers and the dart of a trout in the clear waters. In winter at low tide dunlin, sanderling, ringed and grey plovers may be found patrolling the vast flats.

River Camel, near Old Mill cove

Amazing facts

Eelgrass is the only marine flowering plant that grows entirely underwater.

The Fal Estuary is the third deepest natural harbour in the world.

Despite its name, the oyster-catcher doesn't eat oysters, but devours large numbers of cockles every day.

Oysters are traditionally dredged in the Fal Estuary but all boats have to operate under sail alone – no engines allowed.

Maerl, an incredibly slow growing, red, calcareous seaweed is found in the Fal estuary where it forms the largest beds in England and Wales.

Remains from coastal Celtic settlements show that oysters have been collected for food as far back as 3rd century BC.

Little egrets are rare nationally but Cornwall supports a thriving population.

Eelgrass

Oystercatcher

Nursery grounds

Estuaries in Cornwall are vital nursery grounds for bass. Every winter bass breed in offshore waters and the young form huge silver shoals and head into estuaries to feed on the plentiful resources found there. Bass are predatory fish, feeding on crustaceans, fish, squid and marine worms. The Helford Estuary has a diverse collection of marine worms and these provide a major staple for the growing fish. However, bass are slow-growing and a major cause of population decline is premature capture by fishermen.

There is a minimum landing size of 37.5cm and between May and December all bass must be returned to the water alive.

Bass

SEASONAL INTEREST

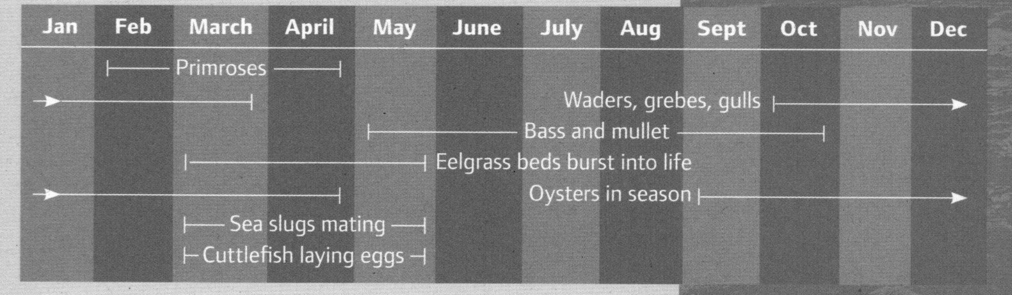

Heathland

The UK has about 20% of the world's remaining heathland: a habitat historically being lost at a faster rate than tropical rainforest. Heathland is an important habitat and characterised by the presence of plants from the heath family, gorse, scattered trees, scrub and patches of bare ground.

Despite looking wild, heathland is in fact manmade. Around 4,500 years ago huge areas of woodland were cleared to provide land for hunting, grazing and agriculture. This heavily grazed land became heathland. Untouched it would revert to scrub and then woodland but continued grazing and burning allows the typical vegetation of heathers, gorse and grasses to remain.

Since 1945, Cornwall has lost 60% of its heathland. This is mainly due to the spread of intensive agriculture eating away at the productive edges of the moors. Modern livestock breeds are less hardy and so cannot be left to roam as widely or as long. This allows the widespread invasion of bracken and scrub. Other areas have been lost to china clay pits and conifer plantations.

The Lizard

The Lizard is the most southerly tip of mainland Britain; a place that remains wild and astoundingly beautiful. This highly exposed peninsula has poor and varied soils produced by the extraordinary geology, meaning the land was never intensively farmed and remained relatively untouched. Here is the largest area of heath in the county, much of the land is part of The Lizard National Nature Reserve, or owned by the National Trust and grazed by old varieties of livestock such as Soay sheep, Shetland ponies and Highland cattle. This controlled grazing has meant the heathland and clifftop grasslands have been restored to nature abounding with wildlife.

What's about?

The most spectacular heath species here is the Cornish heath in July and August. See its glorious blooms across Goonhilly Downs, around Kynance Cove and south of Mullion. Cornish heath looks best with the turquoise sea shimmering behind. Growing with the heath are burnet rose that shelters from the wind behind western gorse, the striking purple betony, heath spotted-orchid, the magenta flowers of bloody cranesbill, milkwort, dropwort, and red and yellow bartsia. The Lizard is also the first landfall for many migratory birds and butterflies. The infrequent but unmistakable monarch butterfly, with burnt orange wings and black edging, might be a surprise visitor in late summer. Another rarity, the chough, emblem of Cornwall, has recently returned to nest on the Lizard after last breeding in Cornwall in 1952. A bright red bill distinguishes the chough from other members of the noisy crow family.

DON'T MISS...

Carpets of heather cover Cornwall and produce a succession of cheerful blooms. First to flower in early July is the bell heather, with tall pink flowers. Following this the pale purple flowers of the common heather or ling burst out. Where it's damp underfoot you might find cross-leaved heath. Feel its downy grey-green leaves and the pink-mauve flowers should still be flowering in October.

Rarities are the Dorset and Cornish heaths with Cornwall being a UK stronghold for both. Plantlife, the wild flower charity, recently voted the Cornish heath Cornwall's favourite wild flower in their survey of UK wild flowers.

WHILE YOU ARE HERE...

Have a look at the Predannack Cliff coastal grassland. The National Trust has managed this land since 1982 and it is one of the first grassland restoration schemes in the county. The Satellite Earth Station at Goonhilly is a major land user and illustrates how modern technology and nature exist side-by-side.

GETTING THERE

Truronian runs a bus service to The Lizard from Truro and Helston. There is a National Trust car park at Kynance Cove (SW 688132) with a viewpoint accessible to wheelchair users. Other car parks can be found at Mullion Cove (SW 667181) that has public toilets and Predannack Wollas (SW 668161).

USEFUL CONTACTS

RSPB Cornwall Chough Project, (01326) 291232.

GETTING THERE

Park at Porthtowan (SW 693480), Chapel Porth (SW 697495), both with car park, café and toilets, or Wheal Coates (SW 703500) which is accessible from the car park by wheelchair users.

USEFUL CONTACTS

Cornwall Industrial Discovery Centre, (01209) 315027.
Blue Hills Tin Streams, St Agnes, (01872) 553341

The Heath Project
c/o Camborne Pool Redruth Urban Regeneration Co. Ltd.
Camborne, (01209) 715424.

Heath spotted-orchid

Chapel Porth

Chapel Porth and St Agnes

Ruined engine houses make the cliffs between St Agnes and Porthtowan a spectacular sight. The prevailing wind comes straight off the ocean and shapes the heathland into waves. This stretch is a relic of the great band of heath that ran right across Cornwall all the way down to The Lizard. Mining was the major source of income on this stretch of coast, with the heather and gorse well suited to the shallow acid soil conditions produced by mining. Following the collapse of the mining industry and the drop in population, the coastal land was abandoned as being poor quality, very exposed and poisoned. Intensive agriculture moved inland and the heathland was lost.

What's about?

While the heavy seas beat against ancient cliffs, listen to the shrill calls of skylarks and meadow pipits. Admire the soaring of ravens, buzzards and the hunting speed of peregrine falcons.

No Cornish heath is found here, but see if you can identify the other four species. Smell the coconut and pineapple of common gorse in spring and the shorter western gorse in late summer. Alongside the footpaths and on bare ground lousewort may be seen flowering in early summer next to dog violets. An unusual plant that may be found here is dodder. Dodder is parasitic and feeds entirely on other plants such as gorse and heather. Small blue butterflies, our smallest resident butterfly, can be found feeding on kidney vetch and gathering in colonies in late afternoon.

Kidney vetch and thrift

Restored!

At last the loss of this habitat has been stopped and in some places reversed. This process has been spearheaded by The Cornwall Heathland Project and involves effective management of remaining heathland and the more visionary approach of re-establishing heathland, including large areas of china clay land. One example of this succeeding is at Caerloggas Downs, north of St Austell, where a china clay tip has been re-contoured and planted with heathland species.

Plants and animals from the wildlife heyday of the past are returning and it is very difficult to distinguish this re-creation from the real thing. Drive to the top for a spectacular view.

More recently the HEATH Project is aiming to reconnect people with heathlands. The HEATH partnership aims to not only preserve heathlands, but ensure it is once again seen as an economic resource for many local communities.

Gorse

Caerloggas

Amazing facts

'Kissing is in when the gorse is out': Old Cornish saying.

The Lizard Peninsula is second only to Teesdale in the whole of the British Isles for its botanical richness.

More than 20,000 species of insects live on heathland.

Cornish legend says King Arthur was turned into a chough when he met his bloody end. This is signified in the red bill and feet of this noble bird.

Heather

SEASONAL INTEREST

Jan | Feb | March | April | May | June | July | Aug | Sept | Oct | Nov | Dec

- Heath spotted-orchids
- Heather
- Dragonflies and damselflies
- Common gorse
- Western gorse
- Butterflies
- Birds of prey

Industrial

Mineral exploitation began in the Bronze Age. Until the zenith of the industry in the 19th century the peninsula supplied the metals that drove innovation and development in Europe and there are very few settlements in Cornwall that have been untouched by the race to extract minerals from the ground.

This legacy continues to mould the Cornish landscape and wildlife. Today metal mining in Cornwall is not economic and the mines remain as historical relics only. However, minerals are still extracted in the form of china clay from the St Austell area and slate and granite quarried from Delabole and Delank. At the height of the metals industry in the mid-19th century, 600 engine houses and processing plants were in operation.

By then cheaper ore fields were opening abroad and the industry went into freefall. The population and economy shrank, the works were abandoned and Cornwall was left with the highest proportion of 'derelict' land in the country. This land was not good enough to farm and being relatively untouched became a haven for wildlife.

The value of this landscape is now recognised for its wildlife and mineralogy as well as its history leading to land management changes to preserve and enhance the wildlife of the areas.

St Austell mining community

Lichen

DON'T MISS...

Industrial workings leave many wildlife friendly habitats behind. A complicated landscape of hummocks, hollows, spoil heaps, bare ground, steep slopes, derelict buildings and water tanks all provide homes for wildlife. As time passes more and more species inhabit these environments increasing the wealth of wildlife.

The plants found on this industrial land are generally heathland species but with rare extras present such as mosses, lichens and liverworts that can survive on this contaminated land. Slow-worms and lizards bask on the bare ground but may slink away if threatened. Ravens soar and roost in the safety of the disused buildings, whilst bats hunt at night.

The striking insect life includes the mottled grasshopper, grayling and silver-studded blue butterflies and solitary mining bees.

Mining bee

WHILE YOU ARE HERE...

Visit the Crowns engine houses at Botallack, clinging to the side of the cliff. The mineshafts here extend over 700m out under the sea. The Count House at Botallack, restored by the National Trust, contains photos of the area at the height of the industry. Admire the rocks of Cape Cornwall; here the Atlantic Ocean officially meets the Bristol Channel and porpoises and dolphins feed in the tidal races around the cape. Also, check out the ancient Penwith field systems along the B3306 to St Ives. Some date from 4,500 years ago and are amongst the oldest in the world.

GETTING THERE

The best sites are accessible on foot from this section of the coast path. Park either at Cape Cornwall National Trust car park (SW 353317) signposted from St Just, Pendeen lighthouse or Botallack (SW 351318).

USEFUL CONTACTS

Geevor Tin Mine Heritage Centre, Penzance, (01736) 788662.

Cape Cornwall

North Penwith Orefields, St Just, Botallack

Spectacularly situated on the coast between Cape Cornwall and Pendeen Lighthouse are tin and copper mines clinging to the cliffs. Here the mineral rich lodes run almost vertically, but tail off a short distance inland. The mines, 100m above the waves, drained easily to the sea for the first part of the works. Deep mining began later with the development of the steam engine in the 18th and 19th centuries. Engines pumped water out and lifted men and ore up the shafts. These engine houses, built for strength, stubbornly remain perched precariously on the clifftops. After the collapse of the industry in the late 19th century the population fell. Nothing could be done with the land that remained and as such the survival of mining relics is exceptional. As the heathland flora merges effortlessly with the scattered industrial remains, the salty sea breezes assault the shore, gradually moulding the landscape this way and that.

What's about?

Because of the metal contamination and extreme coastal location the wildlife present is a somewhat bizarre mix of coastal grassland, heathland and scrub species. The acid-loving gorse and heathers are most abundant along with salt tolerant thrift, common bent and various eyebright species, which are semi-parasitic, gaining nutrients from clovers and plantains. Birds of prey are likely to be seen in this area with peregrine falcons and kestrels the most common.

Salt tolerant thrift

Minions and the South Phoenix Mine, the Cheesewring

Cheesewring tor

The village of Minions is the highest in Cornwall. Within a half mile of the village the labour of millennia can be seen in the landscape: from early mining to the Victorian industrial age. Close by are three stone circles dating from 1500BC and a wind sculpted granite tor. Just to the west of the village centre, a footpath marks the way toward the Hurlers. One significant and two indistinct stone circles make up this ancient site. Local legend says that they are men turned to stone for playing hurling on a Sunday. Near the circles, in a slight dip, the lumpiness of the ground indicates that this was a site of tin streaming, the most basic and ancient kind of mining, where the tin rich gravels were dug from the river bottom.

Head north towards the hill and the Cheesewring tor and a line of pits along an ore-rich vein mark the next stage in the evolution of mining, when men first started to go underground. Once at the top of the tor the final chapter in Cornish mining can be traced. Victorian engine houses lined up along a lode betray the mineral wealth beneath. Here, also, a great granite quarry has been carved out of the hillside. Today it is derelict and only used by climbers and picnickers.

What's about?

It is noticeable that the characteristic heathland flora is found inside the fences that prevent sheep falling down the holes. It is absent elsewhere due to over-grazing, highlighting the complexities of wildlife land management. Important early colonisers of metalliferous mine waste are the lichens, mosses and liverworts (bryophytes). In some places contamination is so severe that little ecological succession takes place and these highly valued pioneers remain.

Many of these Cornish bryophytes are extremely important nationally and internationally. Some are unique to Britain, such as the greater copperwort and some unique to Cornwall including the Cornish path moss. The bird-life in this part of Bodmin Moor is diverse and lapwings and skylarks may be found. Skylarks can be identified by continuous warbling and strange vertical flight.

WHILE YOU ARE HERE...

Visit the South Phoenix Mine to the east of the village that has been restored and is open to the public. Also, be sure to visit Golitha Falls National Nature Reserve (SX 222682), a very beautiful series of rapids in glorious woodland teeming with wildlife, on the road from Minions to Doublebois. Golitha has a car park and toilets.

GETTING THERE

Minions is found off the B3254 from Liskeard (SX 262712). Parking is easy and the village with pubs, shops and toilets is only a short walk away.

USEFUL CONTACTS

Tolgus Tin (tin-streaming works restoration), (01209) 215185.
Cornwall RIGS Group (geological conservation), c/o Cornwall Wildlife Trust, (01872) 273939.

Sea ivory (bushy lichen)

Lichen on a granite rock

Amazing facts

The Cornish suite of minerals, 440 different types, represents nearly 15% of the worldwide total of recognised minerals.

130 of these were first found in Cornwall.

The main ores extracted here were tin, copper, tungsten, lead, iron, arsenic, antimony and zinc, with a little silver and gold.

Granite from Cornwall is known for its great strength and was used in many famous lighthouses such as Eddystone, Bishop's Rock and Beachy Head and Tower and Blackfriars bridges in London.

Today you will have used several products with china clay in them: as well as ceramics such as plates, cups and lavatories; tyres, plastics, paper and medicines all contain clay.

China clay pit

Creatures of the night

Horseshoe bat

Bats are creatures of myth and mystery. However, they are an important feature of Cornish wildlife and are well protected by conservation groups and the law. Cornwall is blessed with a healthy bat population including a few rarities such as the greater horseshoe. These night-flying mammals feed on insects located using high-pitch sound pulses. Deserted buildings right across the county provide day time roosts for these animals; the favourite haunts being old mines, farm buildings and churches. As bats mostly fly at night it is very hard to identify them. Usually, the only clue to their presence is a high pitch chattering and a dark flash or beat of a wing as they speed past on their hunting missions.

SEASONAL INTEREST

Jan	Feb	March	April	May	June	July	Aug	Sept	Oct	Nov	Dec

- Common gorse (March – May)
- Western gorse and heather (Aug – Nov)
- Lizards and slow-worms active (April – Oct)
- Greater horseshoe bat (Jan – Dec)
- Raven acrobatics, peregrines nesting (March – May)

Woodlands

The Cornwall of old was blanketed in woodland before the arrival of man. Remnants of this prehistoric wood cling to survival on the steep slopes of coastal valleys and estuaries.

DON'T MISS...

These temperate rainforests are damp, dark, lush places and over centuries have developed rich wildlife communities and habitats. Most contain nationally, and in some cases internationally, important species of flora and fauna. Western oak woods are beautiful at any time of year, but are particularly stunning in spring from mid-March until May when a succession of wild daffodils, primrose, bluebells, wild garlic and wood anemone carpet the ground.

Ferns are best from spring to autumn, fungi in autumn and birds all the year round. The stunning bluebell is considered rare in Europe and yet in Cornwall they are very abundant. This is primarily due to the life-cycle of the plant and the favourable damp climate and prolonged spring Cornwall offers. In spring expect to see great swathes of blue under ancient woods, in hedgerows and cliff tops.

Lichen and bluebells

The steep-sided wooded valleys were unsuitable for farming and so the wealth of wildlife was left untouched by axe and plough. These conditions are perfect for mosses, ferns and lichens, which shroud the surfaces of rocks and trees. A critical element of these woods is deadwood: the dead trees and branches, both standing and fallen. Deadwood is invaded by fungi, which breaks down the hard, woody material. This makes the wood edible for insects, which in turn are eaten by other insects, birds and mammals.

Fungi growing on a great oak

Two fine examples of Cornish western oak woodlands are Kilminorth Wood near Looe on the south coast and Minster Wood in the Valency Valley near Boscastle on the north coast. Both have similar histories in that they were managed as coppice woods, primarily for their bark. Coppicing is the regular cutting of trees for their re-growth; for oaks the cycle was approximately every 25 years. The bark was used in the tanning of leather and the wood converted to charcoal for fuel. The practice of coppicing mostly died out early in the 20th century, but is being revived in some parts of the country as a way to manage woodland for maximum wildlife interest. Typically, a wood is divided into lots that are cut in rotation, the wood removed and sold as charcoal or poles for fencing. The different ages of wood and different levels of light reaching the ground allows for a thriving wildlife community.

Kilminorth Wood

This remarkable woodland is situated on the steep western bank of the West Looe River and has been wooded for many centuries. Kilminorth is designated a Local Nature Reserve because it typifies the wooded valleys of south coast rias, is one of the largest western oak woodlands in the region and is open all year.

There are many trails that run through the range of habitats to be found within Kilminorth and these offer comfortable wildlife discovery. Whilst here, locate the Giant's Hedge, a massive defensive earth bank running approximately 15 miles from Lerryn to Looe. There is some debate over the age of this bank but estimates range from 600AD to 600BC and it possibly marked the boundaries of a small, ancient kingdom. On entering the wood an information board identifies its location and a map of the woodland.

What's about?

Kilminorth is almost entirely made up of sessile oak, hazel and holly and has a damp lush under-storey that is incredibly varied. Colourful heather cushions dominate in places and elsewhere ferns are prevalent. This variety is caused by changes in soil acidity and light levels penetrating the dense canopy.

Regular coppicing provides feeding opportunities for small mammals in the warm clearings, which in turn attract predators such as the peregrine falcon.

Near the river the wood is dark and damp and this is where the fantastic collection of mosses, lichens and ferns thrive. A wide array of river birds can also be found here including the dashing kingfisher. In late summer and autumn the fungi show, including the stinkhorn fungus, notable by a spongy white stalk and dark bell shaped cap.

WHILE YOU ARE HERE...

Explore the ancient fishing town of Looe, the coast path and the rocky shores and beaches of this part of the coast which are teeming with wildlife.

GETTING THERE

Train to Liskeard on the mainline into Cornwall and catch the bus to Looe. By car Looe is reached on the A387 and pay and display parking is available at the wood entrance (SX 251537).

USEFUL CONTACTS

Looe Discovery Centre, (01503) 262777.

Devichoys wood

Kilminorth wood

Ferns and moss

WHILE YOU ARE HERE...

Explore the ancient harbour of Boscastle and walk the dramatic coast path to Tintagel, the legendary birthplace of King Arthur. In the summer months puffins live on the cliffs and islands along with shags and guillemots.

GETTING THERE

Boscastle (SX 096915) can be reached by bus from most North Cornwall towns. By car Boscastle is reached on the B3266 off the A39, Atlantic Highway.

USEFUL CONTACTS

Boscastle Visitor Centre, (01840) 250010. National Trust Area Wardens Office, (01288) 33137.

Minster Wood

East of the main car park in Boscastle on the south side of Valency Valley is Minster Wood. This strip of coast is very important for wildlife and there is an abundance of steep sided valleys feeding back from the rugged coast. Some of these valleys are wooded and others are rich mixed grassland, but all are of superb wildlife value. With effective management, under National Trust ownership, the wildlife and heritage of this extraordinary stretch of coast will be preserved and enhanced. Minster is one of the very finest western oak woodlands in Britain, with internationally important ferns growing in the damper areas and epiphytic lichens covering the tree trunks.

What's about?

Walk to the river and find dippers, little bobbing birds that dive under the rapidly flowing water to prey on insects beneath the rocks. In the isolated church of Minster at the top of the wood the bell tower shelters a colony of the rare greater horseshoe bat. Some of the less obscure ferns are the hart's-tongue, broad buckler and the dainty Tonbridge filmy fern. Most spectacular of all is the royal fern, sometimes reaching three metres in height, towering above all others. Spot the lungwort lichen clinging to ash and sycamore trees. It was so named because its growth resembled lungs and our ancestors used it as a cure for respiratory ailments.

Dipper

Amazing facts

Dizzard woods

At Dizzard Point, Crackington Haven, there is an oak wood with 150-year-old trees that are only two metres high due to the extreme coastal exposure: natural bonsai!

Oak trees have approximately 450 associated plants and animals, many more than any other British tree.

Britain's oaks have been known to live for more than 1,000 years.

Oak forests rely on jays to distribute their seeds. Jays collect acorns in autumn and fly them some distance away before burying them as a winter cache of food. Most are eaten but some are forgotten and grow up to become mighty oaks.

Oak

Raptors!

All around Cornwall the unmistakable sights and sounds of birds of prey can be found. The agile sparrowhawk manoeuvres between trees in woodland. Keep an eye out on road journeys for buzzards soaring over road verges or perched precariously on telegraph poles. Around the coastal cliffs the graceful peregrine falcon can be seen hunting smaller birds on the wing. This is the fastest animal on the planet, reaching speeds of over 150mph in its stooping dive. If you spot a bird hanging in the sky over road verges or scrub it is almost certainly a kestrel. The ability to hover, excellent eyesight and agility results in a very effective predator. In winter on heath and grassland sites the hen harrier may be found and when dusk falls listen for the distinctive calls of our many owl species. In derelict buildings and churches across the county the pale-fronted barn owl may be found. Unlike the tawny owl, barn owls do not hoot, rather they hiss, snarl and produce a loud clicking noise and so they are easily identifiable.

Barn owl

SEASONAL INTEREST

Jan | Feb | March | April | May | June | July | Aug | Sept | Oct | Nov | Dec

Snowdrops
Primroses
Daffodils, anemones, bluebells
Ferns
Birds
Coppicing
Fungi

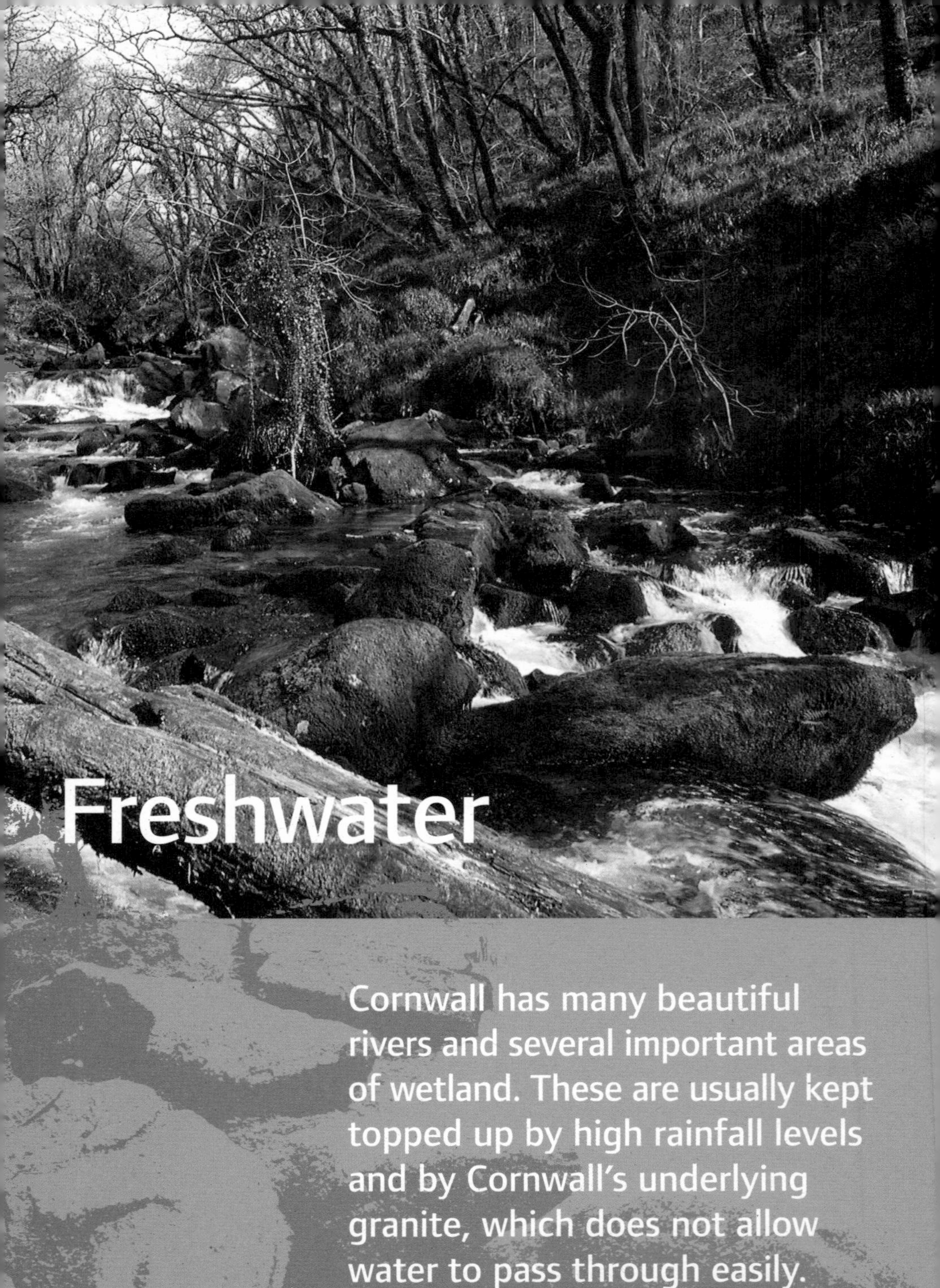

Freshwater

Cornwall has many beautiful rivers and several important areas of wetland. These are usually kept topped up by high rainfall levels and by Cornwall's underlying granite, which does not allow water to pass through easily.

Golitha falls

Damselfly

The wetland areas consist mainly of wet grassland, carr (boggy woodland) and reedbeds and these natural sponges are important for wildlife and regulating river flows. Man has helped shape many of Cornwall's rivers, lakes and wetlands. Most Cornish rivers have been exploited for minerals at some time, with men digging the ore-rich deposits from riverbeds, and are still impacted today by metal-laden discharges from old metal mines and the china clay industry. Cornish lakes are mainly manmade reservoirs on high ground. More recently, wetlands have been drained for agriculture and development, causing dramatic habitat loss for wildlife.

Reeds

DON'T MISS...

Wetlands provide some of the richest areas for wildlife in Cornwall, possessing glorious biodiversity. Bogs are valuable for plants such as sphagnum moss and the insectivorous round-leaved sundew. Amongst marshes and reedbeds look and listen for birds such as grey heron, little grebe, spotted crake or water rail, which makes an odd assortment of groans and screeches.

In summer colourful dragonflies hawk and dart above streams and moorland pools hunting insect prey. The upland lakes, such as Colliford, Crowdy and Stithians, support important numbers of birds that overwinter in Cornwall or stop briefly on long migrations. Smaller ponds and pools are just as important for amphibians such as frogs, toads and newts that need to lay their eggs in shallow water. Rivers are important for the ever-playful otter, now making a comeback in Cornish rivers, and also common birds such as the grey wagtail. This active little bird flits tirelessly up and down the river looking for insects to feed on.

Frog

WHILE YOU ARE HERE...

Explore the coast path or simply admire the stunning coastal scenery in both directions. Gweek Seal Sanctuary is about 5 miles away.

GETTING THERE

Catch a First bus to Porthleven or Helston. Access to this area of National Trust land is either via the coast path south-east of Porthleven or through Penrose Estate off the B3304 from Helston (SW 644242).

USEFUL CONTACTS

National Trust Lizard Countryside Office, (01326) 561407.

Yellow horned poppy

Loe Pool, Helston

Loe Pool gets its name from logh, which is Cornish for 'pool' and is the largest natural lake in the county. It is a freshwater lagoon, which was created approximately 800 years ago when a shingle bar formed across the mouth of the River Cober – effectively damming it. Today the shingle bar is nationally important both for its coastal landform and wildlife. The dry conditions mean that only specialised plants and invertebrates can live there, including the Cornish sandhill rustic moth that is found nowhere else in the world.

Around Loe Pool are many habitats: reedbeds, marshes, carr, farmland and lakeside woods, which all sustain local wildlife. In the past there was an increase in nutrients entering the water from surrounding agricultural land and sewage treatment works. However, the National Trust and other conservation bodies are working on the problem in the hope of many rare aquatic plants returning.

What's about?
Spot plants such as yellow horned-poppy, sea holly and sea kale. Around the reedbeds you will see large stands of common reed, with other tall wetland plants such as branched bur-reed and hemlock water-dropwort. Deeper in the willow and alder carr of Loe Marsh and the Cober Valley you may discover tussock sedge, yellow loosestrife and the trifid bur-marigold. Frogs provide food for grass snakes in the spring. In the summer brightly coloured butterflies such as the silver-washed fritillary move along the woodland fringes. Otters have been seen in Loe Pool and the feeder streams, and there is a variety of brown trout present that is thought to be unique.

Perhaps most astounding is the bird life, with over 100 species recorded so far. In the winter noisy ducks such as wigeon, teal, shoveler, pochard and tufted duck are common. Rare winter visitors include the glaucous gull, northern divers from Iceland and Scandinavia and brent geese, which come from Greenland and the Arctic. At other times water rail, merlin, kingfishers, gulls, waders and swans can be found. Passing vagrants may be slavonian grebe, ring necked duck or even a wandering osprey. There is a bird hide on the northern shore of Loe Pool accessible by wheelchairs – though some distance from the car park.

Loe bar

Bude Marshes and Canal

Bude marshes

Within walking distance of Bude town centre is Bude Marshes Local Nature Reserve. The Marshes cover four hectares of wet grassland, reed beds, open water drainage ditches and pools located between Bude Canal on one side and the River Neet on the other. Whilst not part of the Local Nature Reserve, Bude Canal offers another two miles to be explored on foot. There are few canals in Cornwall, and even fewer that still have open water such as this. The canal was built in 1825 to transport the calcium-rich sea sand inland to sweeten the acidic soils of the inland farms. The rest of this historic canal to Launceston and Holsworthy has all but disappeared.

What's about?

With little traffic from boats wetland plants flourish along the banks of the canal. The water is alive with whirligig beetles, pond skaters and water snails. Dragonflies patrol the skies above the water sharing space with kingfishers. The wet grassland of the marshes provides cover for voles, mice and shrews, which in turn provide prey for kestrels, short-eared owls and barn owls. The pools and ditches amongst the reeds provide perfect conditions for sedges, rushes, wild angelica and southern marsh orchids as well as frogs, toads and newts. Hiding in the reeds are heron, reed buntings and warblers.

Spring brings the yellow flowers of marsh marigold and the active feeding of grass snakes on frogs and small mammals. As summer arrives the pinks of willowherb and purple loosestrife appear and the air is full of butterflies such as the gatekeeper and sombre speckled wood. In late summer at dusk hundreds of swallows enter the reed bed to feed in a great cloud. Autumn heralds the occasional passing of wading birds such as ruff, whimbrel and green sandpiper. In winter the reserve is home to water rail, snipe and teal. A rarity to Cornwall is the bittern and occasionally this may be found on the marshes. Use the bird hide, near the canal on the south of the reserve, to increase your chances of bird sightings.

WHILE YOU ARE HERE...

Visit the culm grassland sites of North Cornwall and South Devon. These damp grassland communities are internationally important for their wildlife. For much of the year they appear damp and uninviting but during the summer orchids and other wild flowers bloom in unison and the pastures come alive with butterflies and moths. Visit Sylvia's Meadow, a Cornwall Wildlife Trust Nature Reserve (SX 413707).

GETTING THERE

Bude is easily reached by bus. There is a car park next to the Tourist Information Centre near the canal in Bude. Public access is limited to the towpath alongside the canal and the old railway embankment, which crosses the marshes and leads toward the river – this is to avoid disturbance to the wildlife (SS 208060).

USEFUL CONTACTS

NCDC Coast and Countryside Service, (01208) 265645.
Bude Visitor Centre, (01288) 354240.

Dormouse

Wet marshy grassland – great for frogs and wetland birds

Amazing facts

- Cornwall has 5,456km of rivers, 1,000 hectares of lakes, and approximately 2,500 ponds and pools.

- You will find fewer snails and more slugs in the west of Cornwall due to the lack of calcium in the soil, which is necessary for their shell growth.

- You may see frog spawn before Christmas due to the mild Cornish climate.

- The only newt you are likely to see in Cornwall is the palmate newt – the great crested and common newts do not like the acidic conditions arising from the Cornish granite.

Palmate newt

Making a comeback

Otter

Otters are making a comeback in Cornish rivers, lakes and estuaries. From the 1950s to the 1980s otter stocks were in serious decline, but now they are on the up. Their recovery indicates healthy fish stocks, relatively unpolluted water and good riverbank habitat. The best chance of finding an otter is likely to be on the rivers Camel and Fowey. A 'splash' in the water heard by the river bank may be your first clue to the presence of an otter. Keep still and quiet and you might be lucky enough to see this sleek mammal powering through the water hunting for fish or merely playing in cool, clear water.

SEASONAL INTEREST

Jan	Feb	March	April	May	June	July	Aug	Sept	Oct	Nov	Dec

Overwintering birds

Otters

Dragonflies active

Frog, toads and newt spawning

Youngsters emerge

Salmon spawning

Hedges, fields and lanes

The agricultural landscape of hedges, fields and lanes dominates much of Cornwall. Hedges are functional features used by man to define land ownership or help manage animals. They are sometimes remnants of ancient woodlands or are the result of clearing stones and boulders for better grazing. These practical hedges have become an integral part of the countryside scenery and provide a network through the modern agricultural landscape for our wildlife.

Honeysuckle

DON'T MISS...

Look out for badger tracks from their nightly foraging or smell in the air the musty scent of a fox. Hazel hedges support the dormouse, recognisable by its bushy tail and golden colour. Birds such as thrushes, yellowhammer, goldfinches, dunnock, wren and chaffinch all rely on hedges for food, shelter and nesting sites.

These small birds attract the dusky sparrowhawk, sometimes heard by its screeching call as it scours hedges for prey. Different hedge types support very different plant communities. Damp woody hedges provide homes for woodland species such as bluebells, anemone, primrose and the summer-flowering stitchworts. Earth banks provide lush growth of ferns, bedstraws, honeysuckles, roses and clematis whereas plants suited to dry conditions favour stone hedges. These include stonecrop, lichens and the delicate blue sheepsbit. In the height of summer, south-facing hedges adjoining the coast path display a rock garden of alpine-like plants with pincushions of thrift, sea campion and the dainty pink rock sea spurrey.

Originally small in size, fields were for grazing or crop production. The explosion of the mining industry led to a rapid population rise in rural and urban areas and the wealthy built huge estates and new settlements. Converted common land became smallholdings for miners to supplement their income and new farms fed the burgeoning urban population. Before modern day fertiliser use, natural products such as guano, manure and seaweed were spread on the land. There were no artificial fertilisers, herbicides or pesticides and this gave rise to flower-rich meadows and fields of corn intermingled with colourful arable weeds such as poppies.

There are some very distinctive hedges in Cornwall. Their form often reflects their location and underlying geology. The style and structure of the hedge also influences the wildlife present. The Penwith peninsula is perhaps the most stunning of these enclosed landscapes. Here ancient granite hedges enclose small, grassy fields. For the best vantage points walk the coast path between St Ives and St Just. A similar style of hedge is found all along the central spine of Cornwall, including areas such as Bodmin Moor.

On the wild north coast the prevailing winds of the Atlantic have created salt-pruned, sculpted bushes that lean drunkenly inland. These sinuous, shrubby hedges define the rustic nature of Cornwall, while quarried slates create patterned hedges on coastal fringes known as 'curzyway'. In the depths of the Cornish countryside, narrow lanes are bounded by high earth banks with shrubs such as hawthorn, hazel, ash and oak perching precariously on top. These earth banks are faced with local quarried stone such as quartz, slate, greenstone and sandstone.

Amazing facts

- Over 600 plant species, 1,500 insect, 65 bird and 20 mammal species have been recorded as living in hedges.
- Some 2,000 species of invertebrates and 300 plant species are commonly found on extensively managed arable fields.
- There are approximately 30,000 miles of hedge in Cornwall.
- Some Cornish hedges, particularly in West Penwith, have their origins from as early as 2,500BC.

Foxglove

Aliens!

The mild climate and clay soils of Cornwall make it perfect for alien invaders from South Africa and Europe. Throughout spring and early summer the hottentot-fig with bright pink daisy-like flowers covers the stone hedges and cliff slopes of Cornwall. Introduced over a century ago, this alien smothers local flora and requires special management in some areas.

From June to September the pink, white and red flower heads of red valerian nod in the breeze, colonising cracks in walls and rocks. The colour continues in late summer with the monbretia and the mass of bright orange flowers seeming to cover every available inch of hedgerow and roadside verge. But that's not all, these are just three of the aliens running riot in Cornwall. Other notable invasive plants, introduced for their good looks, are Japanese knotweed and rhododendron.

GETTING THERE

Agricultural land covers more than 75% of Cornwall so no individual sites will be recommended. Enjoy your exploration!

USEFUL CONTACTS

Cornwall Hedge Group, Cornwall County Council, (01872) 322000
Cornwall FWAG, (01326) 373 823.

Himalayan balsam

Giant hogweed

SEASONAL INTEREST

Jan	Feb	March	April	May	June	July	Aug	Sept	Oct	Nov	Dec

Bluebells (April – May)
Arable weeds in full bloom (June – Aug)
Red campion (Jan – Dec)
Butterflies emerge (March – April)
Hedges cut (Oct – Nov)
Birds nesting (April – Sept)
Bailing (Aug – Sept)
Crop sowing (Feb – March)
Winter vegetable harvest (Oct – Dec)

Credits

First published 2005 by
Cornwall Biodiversity Initiative.

Text by Charlie David, Gus Grand, Richard Marsh, Brian Muelaner, Dan Ryan, Pat Sargeant, Peter Whitbread-Abrutat and Ruth Williams with advice from many local wildlife experts.

Editor Dan Ryan

Photo credits JB & S Bottomley, P Whitbread-Abrutat, Cornwall Wildlife Trust, P Sargeant, K Boot, V Whitehouse, M Wall, North Cornwall District Council, T Dingle, N Tregenza, C Arperry, D Ryan, J Paton, C Butler, CA Perry, R Williams, J Gray, S Hutchings, D Chapman.

Designed and produced by Gendall, Cornwall.

Printed by Rowe the Printers using vegetable oil based inks onto 100% recycled de-inked post consumer waste paper.

Eden Trust, registered charity number 1093070.

General Contacts

Eden Project
Bodelva, St Austell, Cornwall PL24 2SG
Tel: (01726) 811900 Fax: (01726) 811912
www.edenproject.com

Cornwall Wildlife Trust
Five Acres, Allet, Truro, Cornwall TR4 9DJ
Tel: (01872) 273939 Fax: (01872) 225476
e-mail: webmaster@cornwallwildlifetrust.org.uk
www.cornwallwildlifetrust.org.uk

English Nature
Cornwall & Isles of Scilly Team
Trevint House, Strangways Villas, Truro, Cornwall TR1 2PA
Tel: (01872) 265710 Fax: (01872) 262551
e-mail: cornwall@english-nature.org.uk
www.english-nature.org.uk

The National Trust
Cornwall Office, Lanhydrock, Bodmin, Cornwall PL30 4DE
Tel: (01208) 265950 Fax: (01208) 265959
www.nationaltrust.org.uk

RSPB
South West Regional Office
Keble House, Southernhay Gardens, Exeter, Devon EX1 1NT
Tel: (01392) 432691
www.rspb.org.uk/england/southwest

North Cornwall District Council
Coast and Countryside Service, 3–5 Barn Lane, Bodmin PL31 1LZ
Tel: (01208) 265644
e-mail: countryside@ncdc.gov.uk
www.ncdc.gov.uk

Cornwall County Council
County Hall, Treyew Road, Truro TR1 3AY
Tel: (01872) 322000 Fax: (01872) 270340
www.cornwall.gov.uk

Environment Agency
Sir John Moore House, Victoria Square, Bodmin PL31 1EB
Tel: (01208) 78301 fax: (01208) 78321
e-mail: swcornwall@environment-agency.gov.uk
www.environment-agency.gov.uk/regions/southwest

Cornwall FWAG
Resuggan House, Restronguet, Falmouth, Cornwall TR11 5SP
Tel: (01326) 373823
www.fwag.org.uk